[redacted]

Handwriting practice

Teachers' not

Aims of this book

- To reinforce and develop fine motor control.
- To reinforce a left-to-right directionality.
- To practise the movements necessary in handwriting.
- To establish fine differences in letter strokes.
- To introduce letter joins (top and lower joins) and an understanding of the letters that do not join (b g j p s y x z).

These pages of patterns and letters are to encourage children to practise the movements which make up our writing system. In order to practise further, they could use tracing paper to go over an already completed page or use coloured pencils to go over pencil marks.

Developing handwriting skills

This book contains a series of activities to help children at the initial stage of developing handwriting. It will also be useful to other children who are not yet forming their letters properly.

Correct formation of letters helps children to achieve a fast and legible hand. There is often a dilemma for teachers when they notice children writing a letter incorrectly, but absorbed in their work. Should they stop the child writing and insist upon the correct letter formation, or should they let them finish their writing? Each situation has to be assessed individually, but, on the whole, it is best not to interrupt children who are concentrating on the message they want to communicate. It is better to wait and then offer

a practice p
correct move

Children w become accustomed to incorrect letter formation pose a different problem. They need to spend time re-learning and taking every opportunity to ensure that they finally produce the correct movement without having to think about it.

Posture for writing

- Children should be encouraged to sit well back on the chairs in order to gain maximum stability.
- Children should have their feet firmly on the floor. In a writing corner it may be possible to provide a foot rest (telephone directory) for the smaller child.
- Children should not sit hunched over their writing. This is generally caused by the child being too tall for the chair and table provided. In a writing corner a choice of chairs and table heights could be provided.
- Both hands/arms should be resting on the writing surface. The free hand should be used to control the paper.

Writing implements

- As a rule of thumb, the thicker the barrel of the pencil, the easier it is to produce fine motor control. However, if a pencil is too heavy, then obviously this control is lost. If children are experiencing problems with pencil control, a pencil grip may alleviate the problem. There are a variety of these on the market – some even offer moulded grips which take account of the left-handed, as well as the right-handed child (see LDA and Taskmaster).
- Children do need to experiment with as wide a variety of implements as possible, from wax crayons to felt-tipped pens.

Pen holds

Traditionally, children have been taught to hold the pen between the thumb and the first finger, with the second finger acting as a support. Many children adopt this style very quickly. However, an alternative pen hold has been suggested by Rosemary Sassoon where the pencil is held between the index and the middle finger; this can offer a more comfortable hold and greater pencil control (see *Teaching Handwriting* , Stanley Thornes). Care should be taken to prevent children adopting awkward or tense pencil holds, since this will restrict the speed of their writing as they get older.

Paper position

Young children often prefer to have paper placed directly in front of them, but as they become more confident writers, they should be gently persuaded to move the paper either to the right or left of their body and sloping at approximately 30–40 degrees, according to the hand they use. There is no exact position, but comfort and movement across the page should determine the final position.

Helping the left-hander

- Sit the left-handed child on a slightly higher chair so that she can see over the top of the piece of work. This also gives more freedom of movement.
- If possible, demonstrate letter formation with your left hand.
- A pencil grip can be helpful, as left-handers tend to grip very hard. The pencil grip, by thickening the pencil and preventing the fingers from slipping, does relieve some of the pressure.
- Ensure the child has enough space. He should not be knocking either the wall or a friend.
- Encourage the child to try to hold the pencil farther from the point. This enables the left-hander to see what she has written.
- The paper should be positioned to the left of centre and tilted slightly to the right to give more freedom of movement. Young children often find this rather disturbing, and will need gentle but frequent encouragement.

Main handwriting patterns

There are five main handwriting patterns which will be introduced in handwriting families:

1 r n m h p b

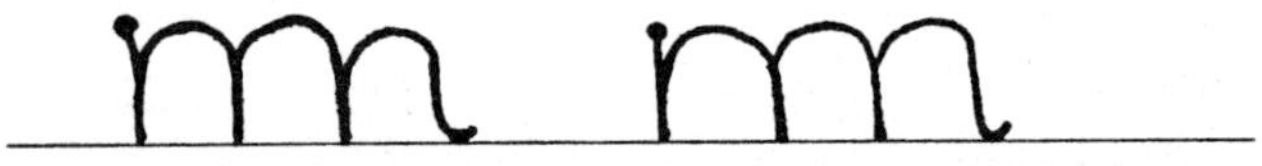

2 i u y l t

3 v w x

4 i u y l t (reinforcing pattern)

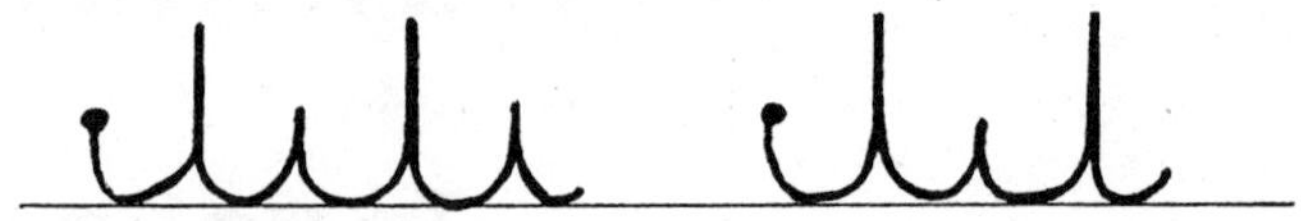

5 a c d g o q

NB Characters e f k j s z are not in a letter family, while some other letters fit into more than one family. It is always worth spending a little time explaining to the children what each activity is trying to achieve in terms of letter formation. Children should not think that handwriting is an easy option, but something which requires work and practice, and of which they can be proud.

Further reading

Essentials for English: Handwriting Patterns, N Gaunt and J Whitwell (1992) Scholastic.
A Practical Guide to Children's Handwriting, R Sassoon (1983) Thames and Hudson.
The Development of Handwriting Skills: a Resource Book for Teachers, C Jarman (1979) Basil Blackwell.
Handwriting: a New Perspective, R Sassoon (1990) Stanley Thornes.
Teaching Left-handed Children, M Clark (1974) Hodder and Stoughton.
Creating a Handwriting Policy, D Bentley (1991) University of Reading.
Joining the ABC, C Cripps (1991) LDA.

Notes on individual activities

General note: Some children might like to colour the activities using crayons. They should be careful not to obscure the patterns.

Notes on pages 5 to 15

It is important to emphasise to the children that they 'start at the dot' and keep the size of writing as consistent as possible. As an alternative, coloured pencils can be used to finish the patterns on the pictures.

Page 5

This is an introductory sheet to practise the five main handwriting patterns. Encourage the children to keep the size of the pattern as consistent as possible.

Pages 6 to 7

These pages introduce the following letters: r n m h p b.

Pages 8 to 9
These pages introduce the following letters:
l u t y.

Pages 10 to 11
These pages reinforce the same letters:
l u t y. However, the pattern changes to emphasise the height of ascenders in letters l and t.

Pages 12 to 13
These pages introduce the following letters: v w x.

Pages 14 to 15
These pages introduce the following letters:
a c d e o q.

Pages 16 to 19
These pages introduce simple joins. Teacher input will be needed to guide and encourage the children in the correct formation of these letters and joins.

Pages 20 to 21
These pages introduce the letters that will join at the top: v w o. Suggesting that the children circle the one they think is best in each line will help them to look at their handwriting critically.

Page 22
This page focuses on joining r and f.

Pages 23 to 24
The two types of handwritten letter k have been separately identified so that schools' handwriting policies can be accommodated.

Pages 25 to 26
These pages identify letters that do not join: s y j b g p. The star at the start of the 'stairs' is to remind the children of left-to-right directionality.

Page 27
This is an individual sheet introducing numbers and number words.

Page 28
This page has been included to show the important link between handwriting and spelling. The teacher needs to use discretion when deciding whether the children are ready to use these letter strings.

Pages 29 to 30
These two pages introduce capital letters. Page 30 introduces the proportion of capital letters to small letters. The pages will also help reinforce alphabet sequence.

Pages 31 to 32
These final pages are exemplars of how lower-case letters, capital letters and numerals should be written. They can be used as teaching aids or traced for use as reminders of the correct formation. If any of the letters or numerals are not the school's preferred style, change or amend them using correcting fluid or felt-tipped pen. 'Start at the top' is still a wise directive to children when teaching them how to write capital letters and numerals, although the forming of these, which have so many more straight lines than the lower-case letters, can be, within reason, left to personal choice.

National Curriculum: English

The activities in this book support the following requirements of the PoS for KS1 for the National Curriculum for English:

Writing
- In **handwriting**, pupils should be taught to hold a pencil comfortably in order to develop a legible style
  that follows the conventions of written English, including:
  - writing from left to right and from top to bottom of the page;
  - starting and finishing letters correctly;
  - regularity of size and shape of letters;
  - regularity of spacing of letters and words.

  They should be taught the conventional ways of forming letters, both lower case and capitals.

Scottish 5 – 14 Curriculum: English language

Attainment outcome	Strand	Attainment target	Level
Writing	Handwriting and presentation	Form letters and space words legibly	A

Watch points for teachers

Tracing patterns and letters can help handwriting.

Joined letters help spelling.

All letters except d and e start at the top.

Capital letters at the beginning of words do not join.

Check sitting position. Both feet should be on the floor, forearm on the table. The non-writing hand should hold the paper steady.

Not every letter has to join!

Un-lined paper, with a line guide makes a reasonable alternative to lined paper.

Regular revision of joins is necessary.

'Do the c first' is a good reminder for letter formation of the a c d g q o family

Check pencil grip. The pencil should not be held too close to the point.

Give lots of praise for effort.

Name ______________________

- Finish the patterns in the boxes, then decorate the page.

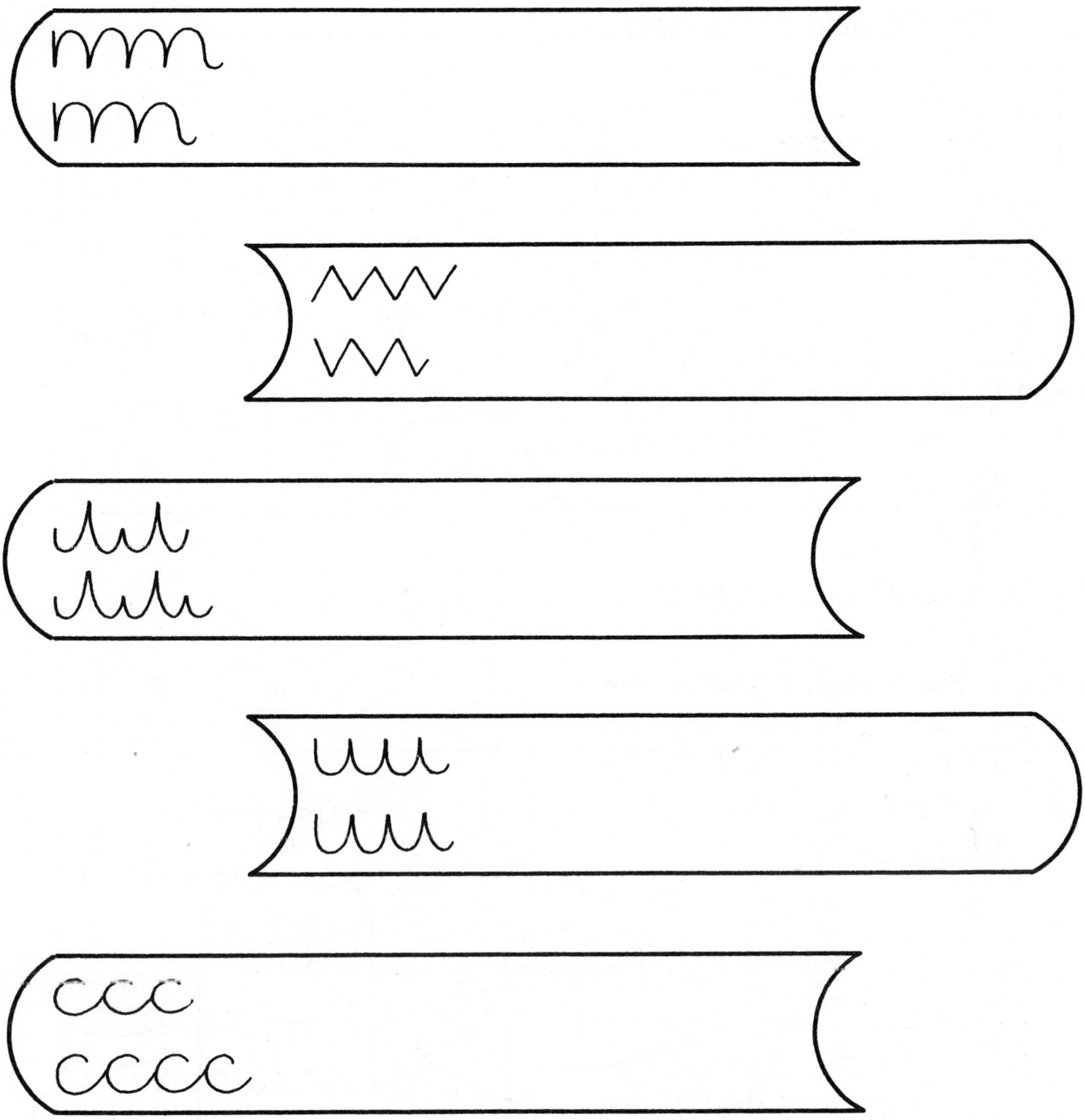

- You make up a pattern.

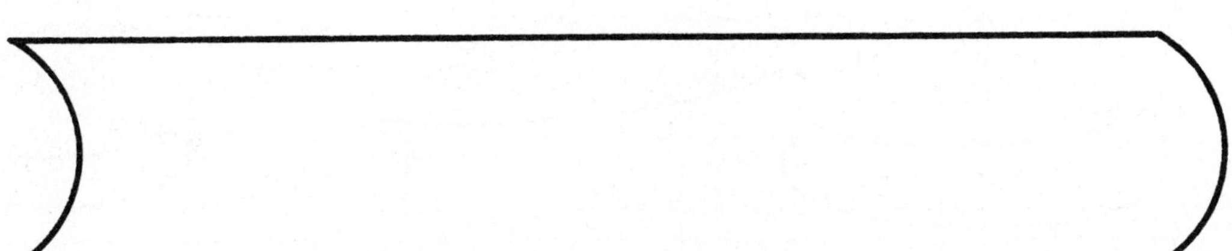

Name ______________________

Go over the patterns and the letters and copy in between. Remember to start at the dot.

mm mm mm m m m

mm n m n m n n n

h h h h mnmh mnh

Finish the lines.

m n h ______________________

h n m h ______________________

Finish the patterns on the jars.

Name ____________________________

● Go over the letters and copy in between. Start at the dot and follow the arrows.

r r r r • • • • r r r r • • • •

b b • • b b • • b b • • b b • •

p p p • • • p p p • • • p p p • • •

● Finish the lines.

r b p ________________________________

b r p ________________________________

● Finish the patterns on the bed cover.

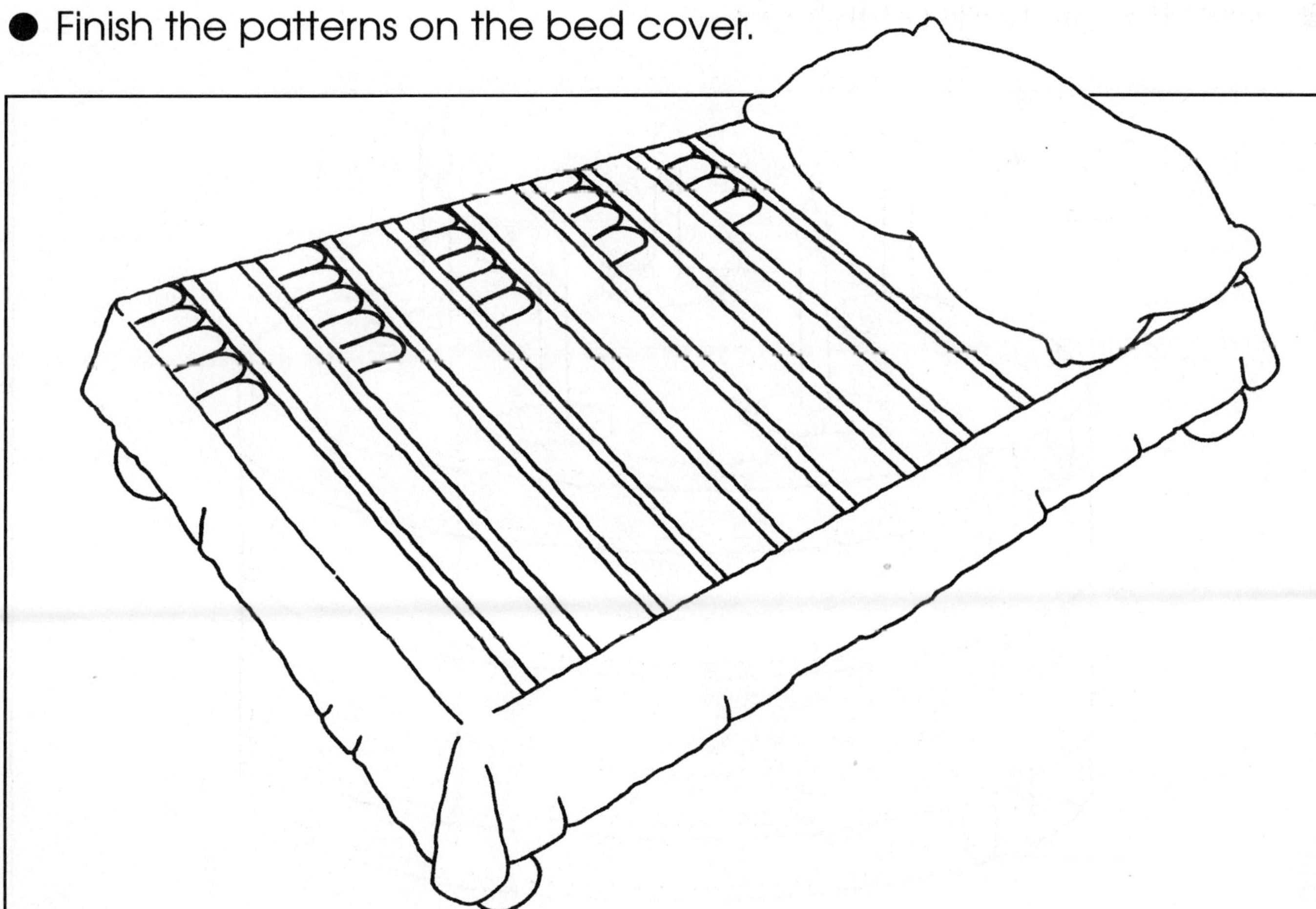

● **Name** ______________________

● Go over the pattern and copy in between. Remember to start at the dot.

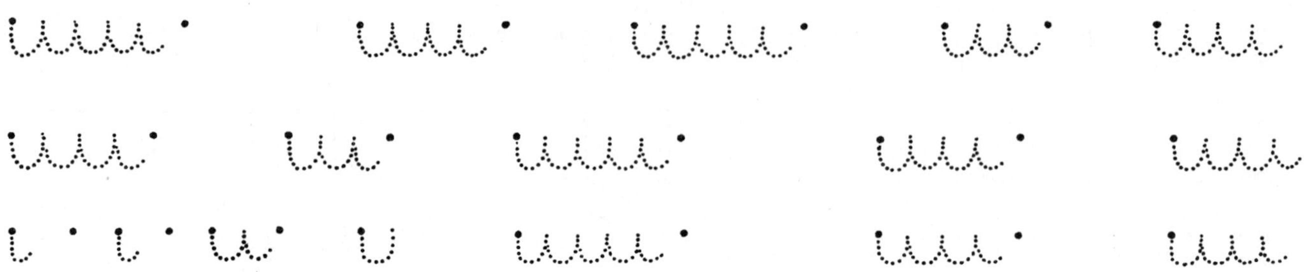

● Finish the lines.

i u i u ________________________________

u u u i ________________________________

● Finish the patterns on the cake.

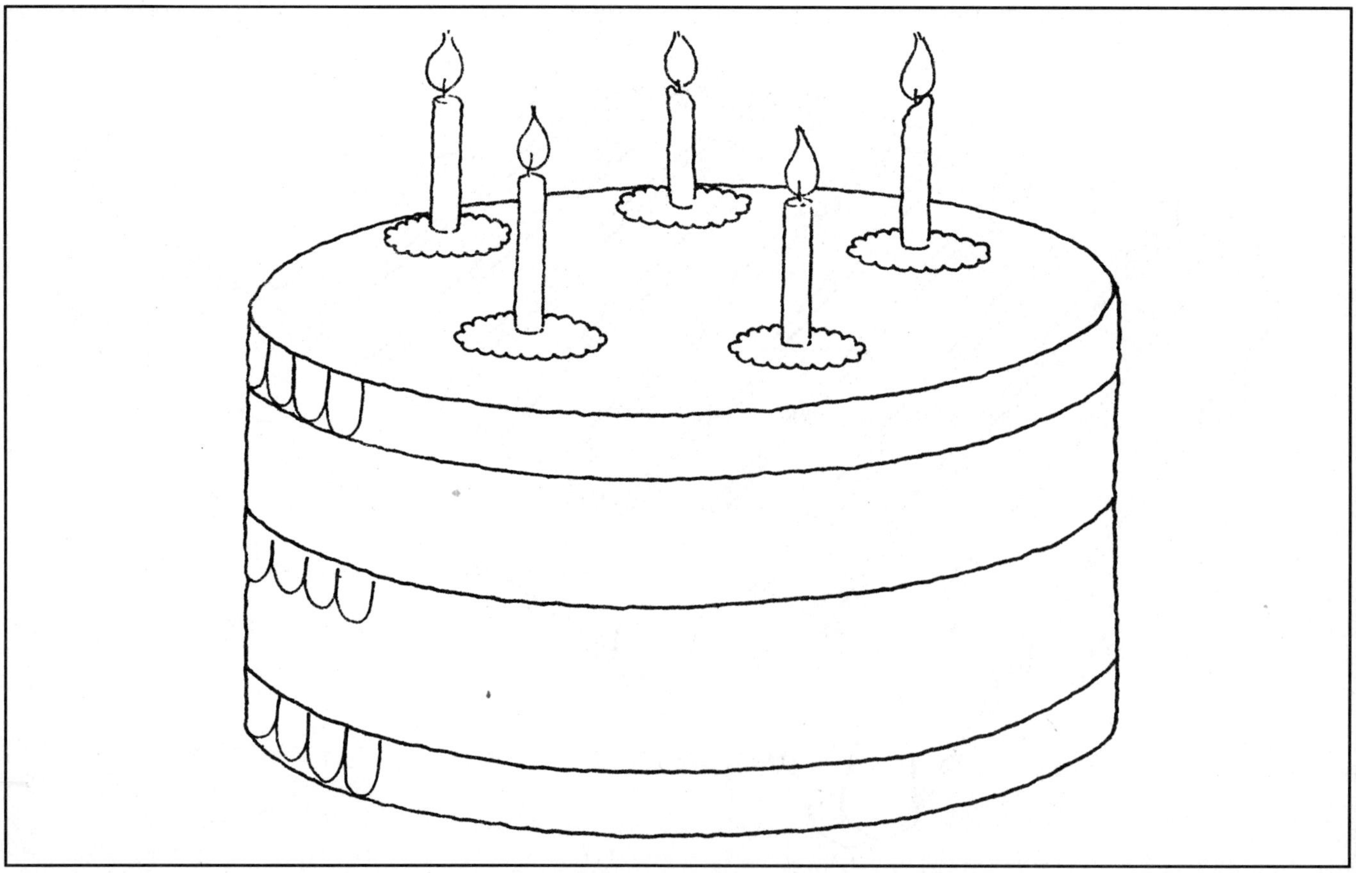

Name ______________________________

● Go over the letters and copy in between. Start at the dot and follow the arrows.

i i i i u u u u u

l l l l y y y y y y y

i l i l y y y i l i l

● Finish the lines.

i l u t ______________________________

y t i u ______________________________

● Finish the patterns on the car.

● **Name** ______________________

● Go over the pattern and copy in between. Remember to start at the dot.

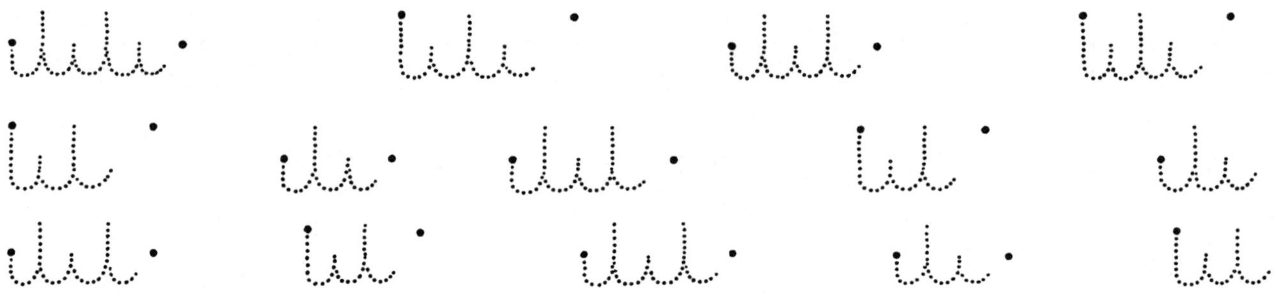

● Finish the lines.

i u l l ______________________

l i u l ______________________

● Finish the patterns on the drums.

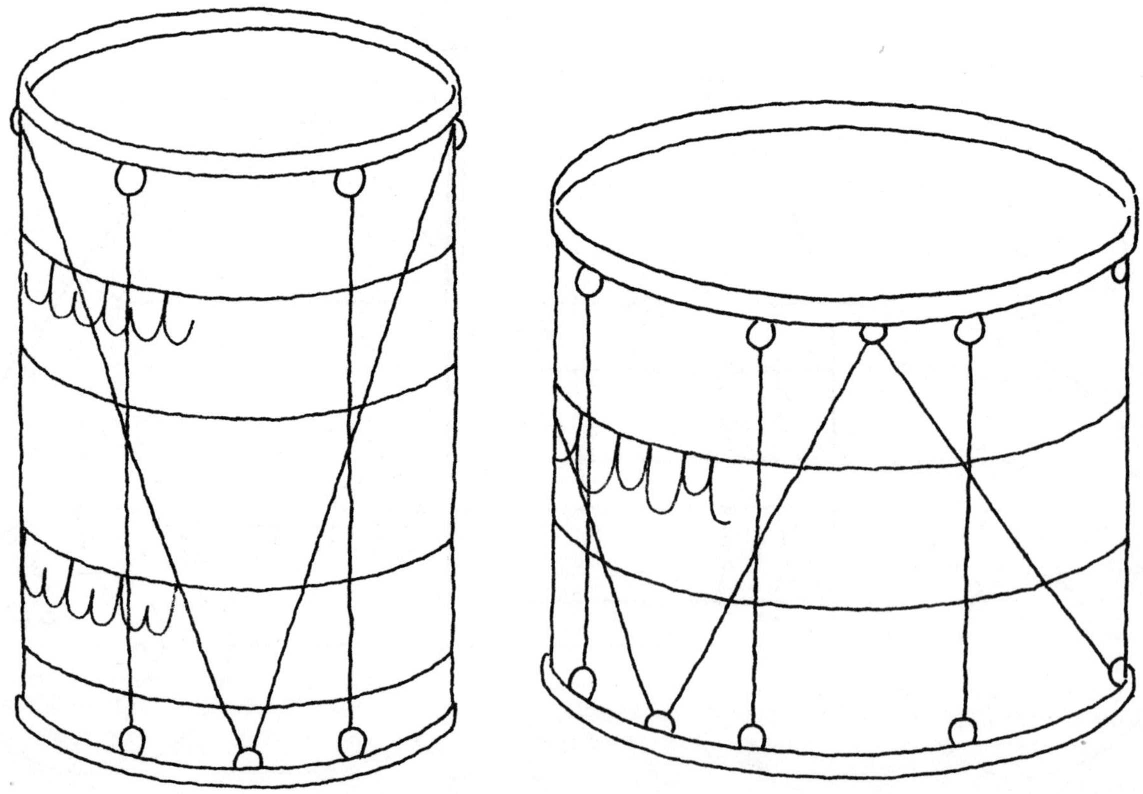

Name ______________________________

- Go over the letters and copy in between. Start at the dot and follow the arrows.

y y y y i i i i u u

y y l l l l t t t t

y y y u u u u u u

- Finish the lines.

y y t t

l t u i

- Finish the patterns on the egg-cups.

● **Name** ______________________

● Go over the pattern and copy in between. Remember to start at the dot.

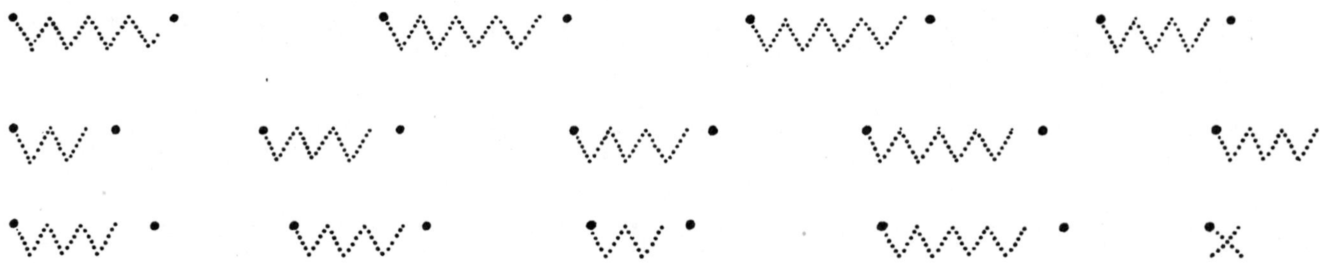

● Finish the lines.

v w x ______________________

w v x ______________________

● Finish the pattern on the lorry.

● **Name** ____________________

● Go over the letters and copy in between. Start at the dot and follow the arrows.

w • w w w • • • w w • •

v v v • • • • v v v • • • v v •

1 2
x x x • • • x x v • w •

● Finish the lines.

w v w v ____________________

v x w ____________________

● Finish the patterns on the tent.

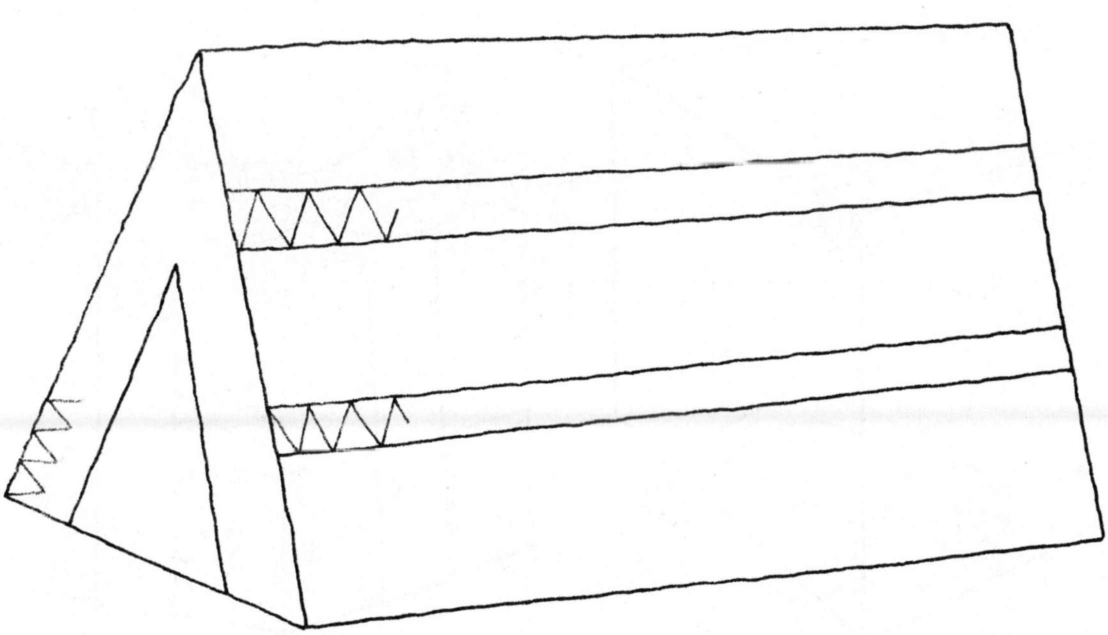

● **Name** ______________________

● Go over the pattern and copy in between. Remember to start at the dot.

cccc • ccc • cccc •

ccc • cc • ccc • cc • cc •

ccc • c c c c c • • • • • •

● Finish the lines.

c c c a a a ______________________

c c a a a ______________________

● Finish the patterns on the presents.

● **Name** ____________________

● Go over the letters and copy in between. Start at the dot and follow the arrows.

a d d • • • • • o o • • o • •

g g g g • • • q q q q • •

a • d • g • o • q o q o d

● Finish the lines.

dd gg ____________________

c o q c o ____________________

● Finish the patterns on the snakes.

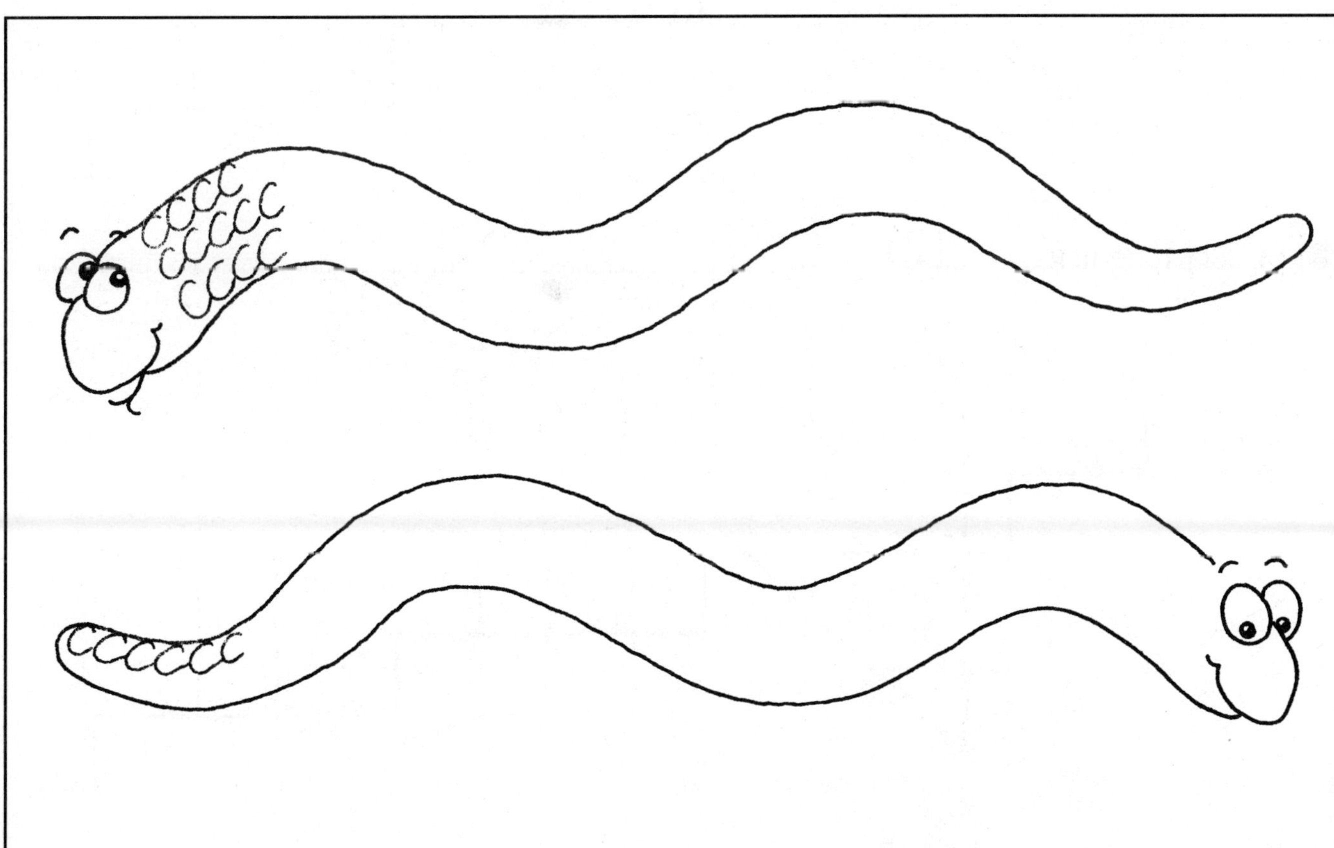

● **Name** ______________________________

● Go over and copy the letters on the stairs. Start at the star*.

*ca ca

ca

cat

cat

● Finish the line. cat ______________________________

*do do

do

dog

dog

● Finish the line. do ______________________________

*la la

la

lad

lad

● Finish the line. lad ______________________________

Name ______________________

- Go over and copy the letters on the stairs. Start at the star *.

*
ac ac

ac

ace

ace

- Finish the line. add

*
od od

od

odd

odd

- Finish the line. odd

*
ea ea

ea

eat

eat

- Finish the line. eat

Name ____________________

- Go over and copy the letters on the stairs. Start at the star *.

* ma ma

ma

man

man

- Finish the line. man

* ho ho

ho

hop

hop

- Finish the line. hop

* one

on

one

one

- Finish the line. one

Name ______________________

- Go over and copy the letters on the stairs. Start at the star*.

* ic ic

ic

ice

ice

- Finish the line. ice ______________________

* da da

da

day

day

- Finish the line. day ______________________

* ru ru

ru

rug

rug

- Finish the line. rug ______________________

● **Name** ______________________________

● Go over and copy the letters on the ladders. Start at the star*.

*

wa wa
wa
wa
wa
way way
way

*

wi wi
wi
wi
wi
win win
win

*

we we
we
we
we
wet wet
wet

● Finish the lines.

● Circle the one you think is best on each line.

way ______________________________

win ______________________________

wet ______________________________

- **Name** ____________________

- Go over and copy the letters on the ladders. Start at the star*.

*

wo wo

wo

wo

wo

won won

won

*

va va

va

va

va

van van

van

*

ve ve

ve

ve

ve

vet vet

vet

- Finish the lines.

- Circle the one you think is best on each line.

won ____________________

van ____________________

vet ____________________

Name ______________________

f and r are special letters. r needs a dip at the end, then it joins easily.

- You try: r r r r ______________________

ra ra ______________________

re ______________________

ri ______________________

ro ______________________

ru ______________________

- Try these words. ran red rib rob rub ______________________

____

f only joins sometimes.

- You copy:

fa fa ______________________

fe ______________________

fi ______________________

fo ______________________

fu ______________________

- Try these words. fan fed fin fog fun ______________________

____

● **Name** ______________________________

Here are some words with 'k' in them.

● Copy the words and find some more.

kick kick

lick

kind

keep

like

bike

kick

● Find some more!

● Finish the lines.

● Circle the word in each line that you think is best.

trick ______________________________

duck ______________________________

luck ______________________________

● **Name** ______________________________

Here are some words with 'k' in them.

● Copy the words and find some more.

kick kick

lick

kind

keep

like

bike

kick

● Find some more!

● Finish the lines.

● Circle the word in each line that you think is best.

trick

duck

luck

Name ____________________

Some letters do not join.

- Go over and copy the letters on the stairs. Start at the star *

* bat bat

bat

bat

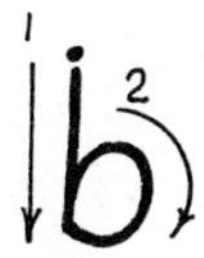

bin

bin

* bin bin

* get get

get

get

give

give

* give give

* put put

put

put

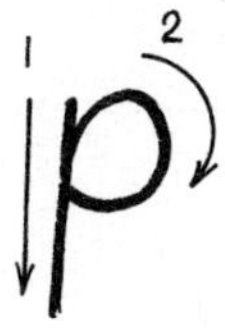

pin

pin

* pin pin

● **Name** ______________________________

Some letters do not join.

● Go over and copy the letters on the stairs. Start at the star *.

* say say
say
say

s

* sit sit
sit
sit

* yet yet
yet
yet

y

* yell yell
yell
yell

* jet jet
jet
jet

j

* jar jar
jar
jar

Name ______________________________

Go over and copy the numbers and the words. Start at the dot.

1 1 1 1

2 2 2

3 3 3

4 4 4

5 5 5

6 6 6

7 7 7

8 8 8

9 9 9

10 10

one one

two two

three three

four four

five five

six six

seven seven

eight eight

nine nine

You finish the line. ten ten

1 2 3 ______________________________

● Name ______________________

● Go over and copy the words.

the

the the
then then
them them
they they
there there

● Can you find any more 'the' words?

ing

thing thing
ring ring
sing sing
wing wing
king king

● Can you find any more 'ing' words?

and

hand hand
land land
stand stand
band band
grand grand

● Can you find any more 'and' words?

Name ______________________________

- Try to keep all the letters the same size.

AAAA ______ A

B ______ B

C ______ C

D ______ D

E ______ E

F ______ F

G ______ G

H ______ H

I ______ I

J ______ J

K ______ K

L ______ L

M ______ M

N ______ N

O ______ O

P ______ P

Q ______ Q

R ______ R

S ______ S

T ______ T

U ______ U

V ______ V

W ______ W

X ______ X

Y ______ Y

Z ______ Z

- Circle the best letter in each row.

● **Name** ______________________________

Here are all the capital and small letters.

A	B	C	D	E	F	G	H	I	J	K	L	M	N	O	P	Q
a	b	c	d	e	f	g	h	i	j	k	l	m	n	o	p	q

R	S	T	U	V	W	X	Y	Z
r	s	t	u	v	w	x	y	z

● Find and write the missing letters.

A	B		D				H		J	K				O	P	Q
		c		e	f	g		i			l	m	n			

			U		W		Y	
r	s	t		v		x		z

● Fill in all the letters.

Name ____________________

- Go over the numbers

1 2 3 4

5 6 7 8

9 10

- Practise the numbers

1	1	2	3	4	5	6	7	8	9	10	
2											
3											
4											
5											
6											
7											
8											
9											
0											

- Lower case letters

a b c d e
f g h i j k
l m n o
p q r s t u
v w x y z

- Capital letters

A B C D E
F G H I J K
L M N O P Q
R S T U V W
X Y Z